Praise for

FAST-DRAFT YOUR MEMOIR

by Rachael Herron

Of all the how-to-write-memoir books I've purchased, checked out, or perused and put back, this book offers by far the most coherent, compact, inspiring, and clear advice.—S. Connor

Rachael Herron resonates with our audience, and not just because she knows her stuff which she does, or because she's hilarious which she is, but because her honesty and earnestness come through in all her messaging.—Samantha Sanders, Writer's Digest

Simply put, if you have ever struggled to finish a book, if you have a yen to write about a time in your life, but aren't sure how to structure it, where to start, how to get through the middle and across the finish line–THIS BOOK IS FOR YOU.—B. Edelman

FAST-DRAFT YOUR MEMOIR WORKBOOK

Write Your Life Story in 45 Hours

RACHAEL HERRON

Text: Rachael Herron
Cover Design: Inspired Designs
Interior Design and Layout: Danielle Smith-Boldt

ISBN: 978-1-940785-59-2

CONTENTS

One

INTRODUCTION

Getting Started!

A Note on Exercises

You are *amazing* for starting on this journey. And clever you, you bought this add-on workbook, which means you're not only amazing, but you're serious about this endeavor. (I already knew that about you. Word gets around.)

And hey! **When I ask you to grab your pen and write something down, I mean it.** Don't be like me. I used to love reading books on writing without doing any of the exercises. Then I got irritated when the magic didn't rub off on me. Seriously, the magic only works when you show up and DO THE WORK. And let me add that you don't actually have to get off the couch (I told you, I see you). Reach for the pen you keep next to the remote and just start jotting all over this bad boy.

Bonus: BOOM! You're writing! Writers write. That's all you have to do.

And doing these exercises count as working on your book!

Important Reminders

- You'll need a copy of *Fast-Draft Your Memoir* (FDYM) to go along with this book. This is merely the awesome space for writing about the things you learn from the text of FDYM.
- Don't leave this workbook out. While the goal of memoir is to tell your ultimate truth, there's nothing wrong with using fake names for your husband or your kids while you're scribbling in this workbook. I won't tell anyone.

1. Write down three huge things you want to share with the world. These can be feelings, experiences, truths you've learned in the course of your life—anything!

2. List three things you're *terrified* of when you think about writing this book.

_____

_____

_____

_____

_____

3. Who might change because of this book? In other words, whose life will this book enhance? This can be either specific people or a certain community (e.g., abused women, recovering alcoholics, cancer patients, people who buy goat farms on a whim).

_____

_____

_____

_____

_____

4. This is why I need to write this book:

5. This is the emotional cost to me if I don't write it:

6. This is what I will let go in order to find time to write it:

Two

WHAT IS MEMOIR, ANYWAY?

A memoir is

- the story of a specific slice of *time* in one's life or
- the story of (or stories on) a specific *theme* in one's life.

A memoir is not

- an autobiography. It's *not* the story of your life!

1. We're going to dive more deeply into what kinds of memoir exist, but ask your gut right now—in which direction are you leaning? (You can't get this wrong.) Do you want to write about a slice of time or about a certain theme? Take your time with this question. Noodle on it for a while.

   PRO-TIP: keep your hand moving without stopping until you fill these three pages. If you run out of things to write, just write, "What should I write next?" until another thought occurs. You might be surprised by what happens!

2. What are you most worried about at this moment? The actual writing? The organization?

3. What's most exciting to you right now about the idea of writing this memoir?

Three

REASONS NOT TO WRITE MEMOIR

You learned in Three of FDYM a few good reasons *not* to write a memoir. I'm sure you're in no danger! And if you are, this workbook is a life preserver, never fear.

For now, let's dive into some things you might *like* to include.

1. List some things you're angry about that you might like to write about in this memoir. (Surprise! Anger is totally appropriate in memoir! It's just the memoir-as-revenge we're trying to avoid here.)

    1. _____

    2. _____

    3. _____

4. _____

5. _____

6. _____

7. _____

8. _____

9. _____

10. _____

11. _____

12. _____

13. _____

14. _____

15. _____

2. Look at your list, above. Which ones do you want to write about because it will convince someone of how right you are? (Be honest. We all have these.) Circle them.

3. How are you awesome? List the ways. (Yes, you *are* awesome! I know this!) Get creative here. Really brag like you've never bragged before, like your paycheck depends on it.

   1. _____

   2. _____

   3. _____

   4. _____

   5. _____

   6. _____

   7. _____

   8. _____

   9. _____

   10. _____

   11. _____

   12. _____

4. Look at the "awesome" list. For each item on the list, can you remember a time you weren't awesome at that thing? Can you remember when it was hard, or when you were terrible at it? If yes, circle the item. Then come back to this page and jot down a list of what happened, and approximately when it happened.

1. _____

2. _____

3. _____

4. _____

5. _____

6. _____

7. _____

8. _____

9. _____

10. _____

11. _____

5. Where is your sadness? Where is your heart broken? What bits will never fit together again because of something or someone you've lost? I know it's hard, but write those losses down in a list, right here.

1. _____

2. _____

3. _____

4. _____

5. _____

6. _____

7. _____

8. _____

9. _____

10. _____

6. If anything on this list brought you to tears while writing it down, circle it.

Okay. Now this part might be hard.

In the anger question, you shouldn't write about your circled items.

You saw that coming, right? You just shouldn't. You *can* write about these items *if* you can be harder on yourself (written with full honesty) than the other person (about whom you will write with compassion). A reminder of why this is important: you'll *never* convince the other person that you were right. Instead, you'll convince the reader that you're a nagging jerk who can't let things go. That's not to say that you should let all things go! Of course you shouldn't! Don't forget, you get to write about *any* anger item as long as you're not trying to convince anyone in your past that you were right and they were wrong. If your mother was abusive, if your husband beat you, you deserve to write about this very real anger. Just know that you can't *ever* change *them*.

7. How do you feel about leaving behind the need to make someone else see your side of the story?

For every item you circled on the awesome list? Guess what? You *do* get to write about your extreme amazingness—at length, if you want!—*as long as you can also show how you started out not being that great at all.*

8. How do you think it will feel to write about the time *before* you got mind-blowingly good at the items on your list?

_____

_____

_____

_____

_____

_____

_____

_____

_____

For the circled items on your sadness list, think about how *hard* you cried. If the tears were uncontrollable, consider waiting a bit longer before writing about these items. Mary Karr says in *The Art of Memoir*, "Can you be in that place without falling apart? If you're sobbing with shoulders shaking and big tusks of snot coming out of your face, the answer may be no. Call a pal, book a massage, go for a walk. You're not ready to occupy this space for years on end. Yet." If, however, you wrote the sad thing down and you were able to keep working, then it might be okay for you to keep writing about this. You are the only person who can make that decision for yourself.

9. What kinds of memories are clear and strong? Certain years? Certain people or places?

10. What are you bad at remembering?

Four

FAMILY: CAN'T LIVE WITH 'EM, CAN'T WRITE ABOUT 'EM

The Safety Circle

- Inside the circle on the next page, put the names of the people you'd trust to read parts of your memoir. They're the ones who won't care what you say, who will cheer you on, who will believe in you one hundred percent (no less!) no matter *what* truths you tell.
- Outside the circle, put the names of the people you'd like to protect your manuscript from while it's in the early stages, while it's learning how to breathe.
- BE BRUTALLY HONEST WITH YOURSELF.

My students are always surprised by where people fall. When I did this exercise for the first time, I included my then-boss in the circle, something that shocked me. We weren't really friends outside the job. We didn't even hang out together, yet I trusted her completely. And my boyfriend, the man I thought I told everything to, was outside of it, which made me feel ashamed. But I knew the Circle was right.

Now, write about what surprised you most on your Safety Circle page.

_____

_____

_____

_____

_____

_____

_____

_____

The People Pages

1. List the names of people you want to include in your memoir, but writing about them worries you.

2. Next to each name on the previous page, list the worst thing they could do if they were to read what you want to write. BE BRAVE. If it's important that they never see this, we can guarantee they won't (more on that in a minute). If your list includes things like, "disown me," or "divorce me and take my children away," or "stab me to death with a broken spork," that's okay.

3. Take a minute to do some journaling. Some of you might have no one listed on the previous page. Others might have twenty people or more. Still others might only have one person listed, but that person feels *really* problematic. (Again, don't worry. In just a minute, I'm going to give you a method that ensures they'll never see these words— but *don't skip ahead* before doing this!) Be brave and write the truest truths you've ever written about them. Use these pages to write out your heart.

Did you do it? Congratulations! I know you *thought* you knew what you felt about this fear, but I also know that you were just surprised by some things that came out of your pen. (Didn't do it? Do it now!)

Now that you've been so brave and written all that emotional, important stuff down, I'm giving you permission (let's even call it encouragement!) to RIP THOSE PAGES OUT AND BURN THEM. And by burn, I mean, yes, take a match to them, but *also* be really safe about it. I'd love to do this kind of thing in a metal rubbish bin in a brick courtyard, but since I don't live in a British manor, I usually burn them in the driveway with a fire extinguisher at hand. (You can take the girl out of 911 fire dispatch, but you can't take the 911 fire dispatch out of the girl.)

Go! Rip! Burn!

UNLESS: you might be one of those people who actually don't mind saving this, knowing that if someone opens your memoir-writing workbook, they get what they deserve. In which case, leave those pages in here! You're right!

On the fence? Yeah, that's where I usually am, too, so I have a clever solution for you! Save *and* burn.

1. Snap a picture of each page with your phone (or scan them if you're fancy).
2. Email the group of pictures to yourself using the subject line, Tax Deduction re: Conservation Easement 1997. This guarantees no one will EVER open that email if they happen to be snooping.

3. IMPORTANT: delete (completely) the pictures. If they auto-upload to the cloud, make sure you delete them there, too.
4. Archive or save this email with its impossibly dull subject line! You'll be able to search for and bring it up anytime you need it.
5. Then burn, baby, burn!

Who Gets Veto Power?

Who in your life deserves veto power? Who are the ones to whom you'd like to show your pages and allow to say Yea or Nay?

Important Reminders

1. While it's great to have these people picked out, *do not let them read your book in full.* They are only allowed to yea or nay the parts with them on the page.
2. Even with those important people, *do not show them a thing* until you're at least three or four revisions in. Not a first draft, and not even a second draft. If this rankles you, reread this whole chapter. Don't let anyone ruin your book for you. It's too precious to risk! Make sure your book is as close to polished as you can make it—like, you're about to query agents or hire an editor—before you show them. Yes, this is dangerous. They could say "Take me out completely!" But you'll be a master reviser by then, and that'll be easy, plus you'll be so irritated with them that their sections will be easy to lift out. They normally don't

say this, though. If you love them so much you give them veto power, they're usually your Trusted Few, and you can, indeed, trust them.

3. THE VAST MAJORITY OF PEOPLE YOU WRITE ABOUT WILL NOT GET VETO POWER. You might not have a single person to grant this power to. That's great. You don't need permission to write about anyone, ever.

So, does anyone get Veto Power in your memoir?

Another Important Reminder

If you feel your memoir *could* be read by someone while you're writing it—if you have a nosy teenager or spouse, or even just a bored one—**password protect your work on your computer right** now. No joke. Do it this instant. You might think you'd be fine if they read your work in progress, but trust me, you won't be, and worse, if you have to defend your writing while it's still barely blushing green, unfurling its careful tips to the warm sunlight, you won't be able to face going back to it. Password protect the file, if not your whole computer. You deserve privacy, and you're worthy of it.

Five

TRUTH AND MEMORY

After worrying about family and loved ones, this is the second-most popular discussion topic in every memoir class I've ever taught.

So let's dive in and get *you* to think hard about what matters to you.

1. What *is* truth? Don't look up the dictionary definition—instead, write down what truth *means* to you.

_____

_____

_____

_____

Rachael's 80 Percent Rule

Review what you learned in Five of FDYM. Now, think about the people who might appear in your memoir. Answer this question of the big players: *What would they say to you after they were in a car accident they caused?*

You know what they'd say. You know them so well! Write a few lines of (fake) dialogue for each character (because in your memoir, they *are* characters).

NAME:

NAME:

NAME:

NAME:

NAME:

NAME:

NAME:

NAME:

Look how well you know how these people talk! Take heart in this. It means when you're writing down things that happened, you get to *recreate* dialogue as if you have a perfect memory!

Conflating Situations/Shifting Time

It can be extremely tedious and not at all helpful to a story's progression to write down every single time things happened, in the exact order in which they happened. Are there things that happened in your life or things that you'll want to change, timewise, in your memoir? Brainstorm about this here. (But it's okay not to be sure! This isn't even a first draft yet!)

Combining/Changing Characters

If you lived with five male roommates who were all studying to be lawyers and who all drank too much on the weekends, for the love of God, don't tell us about each one of them if they're not pivotal to your story. If, back then, *you* could barely tell them apart, we as readers will never have a chance.

Who are minor characters who might appear in your memoir that you'd like to combine into one person?

Disguising Features/Changing Names of Characters

Is there anyone you might disguise in your memoir? Remember—do these changes *after* you write your memoir. If you call Aunt Beezy by a different name and change her hair while you're writing your book, then after a while, this aunt will start to feel fictional to you. Keep her as Aunt Beezy with that wild orange hair until the last possible moment, to keep her as real as you can in your mind.

Mary Karr says, "Truth may have become a foggy, fuzzy nether area. **But untruth is simple: making up events with the intention to deceive.**" [12] [Emphasis mine.]

Don't forget: truth is hard to tell other people about, yes. But you'll know when you're straight-up inventing things that never happened. Don't do that.

Six

WHY YOU SHOULD WRITE QUICKLY

You're going to write badly.

Let me say it again for the ones in back: YOU ARE GOING TO WRITE BADLY. Everyone writes badly in a first draft. If you don't do that, *you won't finish writing your memoir.* (Want to see what my first drafts look like? Go to RachaelHerron. com/sfd for an example!)

Remember what you learned in Six of FDYM: revising as you go is the very worst thing you can do if you want to finish your book.

You can't know what your book wants to be until you've finished a first draft.

Even if you're sure you know, you're probably wrong. Most writers are. You'll never finish a first draft if you keep going back and fixing scenes that might not even earn their spot in a second draft of the book you don't understand just yet!

So let's talk about some of the great writing that you love, that your book will *not* look like at first.

The Gap

You have killer taste. You *love* great books. List your favorite memoirs here. (If at least five beloved titles don't spring to mind, then you need to be reading more memoirs! You can't expect your book to be read and loved if you don't know what other writers are doing, if you don't read and love their work!)

The Gap Vs. Reality

Here's what *will* happen. Your writing is going to let you down. And that's okay—that's normal. So let's set some intentions around how you'll handle those feelings when they crop up. **Don't skip this exercise—it's a really important one!**

1. When you're working and your dastardly little inner editor pops up and says, "You're not a good enough writer to pull this off," what will you say back? (Suggested answers include: *This is a first draft. Back off. Thanks but no thanks.* Write your own!)

_____

_____

_____

_____

_____

2. Brainstorm what you'll do on the days when in your heart and soul you're saying, "I can't do this. It's pointless." These should be *actions* you can take. (Suggestions include: *phone a writing friend for a pep talk, write about the writing in your journal, go for a walk and record ideas about your book.* Now write your own!)

_____

_____

_____

_____

_____

_____

3. List the people in your life you can go to for support.
   They can't read your work yet! Not until it has covers! But
   who will know that you might come to them for a pep
   talk when the Gap feels really un-closeable? (If you don't
   have many on this list, it's time to prioritize creating your
   writing community!)

_____

_____

_____

_____

_____

_____

REMINDER: the Gap is normal. Feeling like you're a terrible writer is so uncomfortable, and most writers feel it every day. We just nod civilly at the feeling and then do some work, anyway. This gets easier and easier with practice.

Doing Your Math

A short memoir can run from 25,000 to 40,000 words. A medium one will be 40,000–80,000 words, and a long one will be anything over that. If you're hoping to take a traditional publishing route, you'll have to aim for the long end of medium or longer. Most traditionally published memoirs are around 90,000 words. If you're thinking of self-publishing, though, you can write whatever length you want!

How long do you want yours to be? Remember that this is just a guess!

Fifteen Minute Mad Dash

This exercise requires the computer on which you do your writing.

Your prompt will be "Home is..." Your stab at this exercise can include describing the last five places where you lived. It can be about a person who means home to you. It can be about the couch that says you're finally off work. It can be about the home you always wanted, or the one you had and lost. If you're writing about one kind of home and run out of words, then *restart the sentence* and chase it.

Now! **Go to your computer** and write for fifteen minutes, as fast as you can. Set an alarm on your phone. *KEEP YOUR HANDS MOVING.* When you run out of things to type (and you will), push yourself to keep going. Lost that train of thought? That's fine! That happens! Jump on the next train and ride it to a different destination.

DO NOT GO BACK AND READ AS YOU WRITE. This is key! You can back up to fix a quick spelling error if you haven't gone more than a word or two past it. But don't read! Don't stop! Keep the hands moving! You can fix everything later!

Yes, you're typing this, not handwriting it, as I assume you'll write your memoir in some kind of word-processing app. (If not, you might not be fast-drafting, but you can certainly still hand-write a memoir.)

And…go!

Your prompt: Home is… **Do this for fifteen minutes exactly. Start now.**

Good job!

Now, we do the math.

Word count = _____

Multiply by 4 = _____

This number is your average rate of words per hour. Don't be alarmed if you're under five hundred words per hour. *Do* be surprised (and brag to a friend!) if you're over a thousand.

More math!

Take the number of words you want your book to be, and divide that by your words-per-hour rate.

Goal word count for your book = _____

Divide by your hourly pace = _____

No matter what, your book's first draft will take about this amount of time!

For example, if you're writing a 60,000-word memoir and your writing pace is 1450 words per hour, then it's going to take you 41 hours to write this book. If you're writing a 90,000-word book with the same pace, it'll take you about sixty-two hours.

It doesn't matter if you spread this over a year or over 90 days, it'll still take you about this long! Isn't that exciting? Now you know!

REMINDER: most people can't write more than an hour or two at a time. It's mentally (and physically) exhausting, so even if your number is on the low end, do *not* try to write for forty hours in a work week—it won't work! Go back and review the Deep Work section in FDYM for more on this.

Seven

TYPES OF MEMOIR

1. Read this list and **draw a star** by the kinds of memoir you love best *to read*.

- **Celebrity, athletic, political, or public figure:** Famous people writing well-paid and well-publicized books, usually ghost-written.
- **Travel:** The story of a trip or trips. *Eat Pray Love* fits into this category.
- **Spiritual:** The story of finding a spiritual revelation. *Eat Pray Love* also fits into this category, immediately proving the fact that it's okay to hit more than one category.
- **Food:** *Julie and Julia* fits in here, as does, you guessed it, *Eat Pray Love*. Is Elizabeth Gilbert just showing off now?

- **Grief:** Joan Didion's *The Year of Magical Thinking* and Sonali Deraniyagala's *Wave* are good examples.
- **Animal:** Yep, there are plenty of memoirs about a pet that was pivotal to a life. I have to admit to a weakness for these, although the end of the book is usually that the animal died, so ouch.
- **Farmsteading/Pastoral:** A person for whom free-range eggs are as close as they get to a farm suddenly ups and moves to the country, preferably with their long-suffering spouse whose subsequent horror can be mined for comic effect.
- **Mommy Dearest/Growing Up Dysfunctional:** These books are full of family pain and are sometimes hard to read. *The Glass Castle* fits here. Take care to add some humor/irreverence, or your reader will want to kill himself with a butter knife by the end.
- **Escape From Religious Extremism:** Sign me up! I'm always down for a cult memoir. Bonus points if the setting is something I'm not familiar with, like a jungle. Or, okay, a church.
- **I'll Take You There (Zeitgeist):** These capture the spirit of a time. Here, care has to be taken to bring the author into the narrative. It's easy to get lost in a Summer of Love memory and talk a lot about Janis Joplin, but Janis (bless her) will never be as interesting to the reader as *you* will be. Front and center, please.
- **I Will Survive (Disaster):** Did you cut off your leg to get away from a rabid panda? This is your genre!

- **Love and Romance:** Guess what fits here? Yep, that damn *Eat Pray Love*. I'm telling you, I'm starting to figure out why this book was as big as it was.
- **Family and Friendship Relationships:** *Let's Take the Long Way Home* by Gail Caldwell, or Ann Patchett's *Truth and Beauty* are good examples.
- **Workplace or Career/business:** Here, the business should be something interesting. If you set out to write the story of your life seen through the Excel spreadsheets you edited, you might be signing yourself up for difficulty (though I'm sure it can be done well in the right hands). But if you train killer whales to be international spies? We sure want to hear about it.
- **Exploration or Adventure:** Did you get lost hiking in Peru? Tell us about what you saw. This can strongly overlap with Travel or Disaster memoirs.
- **Illness:** Your everyday cancer memoir fits in here. Yes, there are lots of them. Yes, agents are tired of getting queried about them. No, that doesn't mean that yours isn't the one the world is waiting for. It's possible that your illness memoir will be the one that helps someone else find their way through, so yes, write it if you're called to it.
- **Addiction/recovery:** Again, sign me up. If you were ever too strung-out on meth to remember to pick your kid up from school, I want to read your book. What? I'm a simple person. I like the reminder that my

problems aren't that bad. Memoir is a great way to be reminded of this.

- **Humor:** Caitlin Moran's *How to Be a Woman*. David Sedaris's whole catalog. Humor isn't easy to write, but I think you know if you're good at it. And if you're great at it, it might be difficult to write anything but.
- **Call to Action:** Often (but not always) political, call to action memoirs are the ones that get you off your ass and talk you into *doing* something. Ta-Nehesi Coates's *Between the World and Me* is a recent stunning example of this.
- **Stunt:** As mentioned in FDYM, when a memoirist does something in order to write about it. Anything by A.J. Jacobs is in this category, like the time he tried to live by all biblical rules for a year, or when he took a year to read the encyclopedia.

   List inspired by and expanded upon from
   Swenson Book Development.

2. Now scan back down the list and CIRCLE the ones that might suit your memoir idea!
3. Do your starred items and your circles align? Great if they do, and equally fine if they don't! What feelings do you have about this?

_____

_____

Eight

PLANNING: PART ONE

Your Six Pivotal Moments

What six pivotal moments shaped you as a human? Yes, only six. No more, and importantly, no fewer. This exercise is about culling down ideas. If you have more than six, decide which had more impact. Your brother's death may not have been as impactful as your grandmother's death—even though that's unexpected, this is about *your* truth. You get to decide what's most important. There's no judging. You won't show this list to anyone else. Be honest with yourself.

PRO-TIP: use a pencil! You might remember something that happened that's actually more important. And you don't have to list them in chronological order!

1. _____

2. _____

3. _____

4. _____

5. _____

6. _____

Okay, got them? Great. Let's move on to the next step!

The Six-Word Memoir

The six-word memoir is a simple form. Your story, in six words. It's easy enough that second-graders understand it, and tricky enough that award-winning poets struggle with it.

Yes, the six-word memoir really is a memoir.

And yes, you can have as many of them as you like, just like full-length memoirs (but the six-word version is practically instant and therefore gratifying).

Examples

- Letters, words, sentences: my life's grammar.
- Make, break, fix. Do it again.
- Arrived with hope, leaving with same.

Write a six-word memoir of your own. If you're stumped, look at your six pivotal moments. Choose one and write about that. If your divorce was a pivotal moment, write a six-word memoir about it, keeping the focus on yourself. *Married too young. Divorced just right.*

Be loose and floppy with your attempt. If your shoulders go high, if your jaw clenches as you furiously scratch out word after word because they're not just right, slow down and take a deep breath. You won't get this wrong. You can't. It's yours. Grab it. Go!

Now, do another one!

And another!

Feeling the rush? Do some more. Write one for every pivotal point, then add a couple more. Finish when you're depleted of ideas, but don't work at this for more than ten minutes.

One of these six-word stories is the one you'll write about for your memoir. Just one. So draw a big star next to the one you think you want to write about.

This will be your focus.

This will be your *book*.

HOW EXCITING!

Nine

PLANNING: PART TWO

Your Big Personal Change

Remember what you read in Nine of FDYM—as the most important character in your memoir, you *have* to change within the covers of your book. It's not optional. And you have to show that change clearly to the reader.

So, look at your six-word memoir. Really think about it. Use your six-word memoir for inspiration. Again, don't spend more than ten minutes on this.

Glance at the book for examples if you need them, and then fill in these blanks:

I started out _____

_____ .

I ended up _____

_____ .

Got it? This is your character arc throughout *this* memoir that you'll be writing. Remember, if you chose to write a different memoir about a different part of your life, that character change would be different. This change is for *this* memoir that you've chosen! Great job!

The Two-Sentence Premise

We're almost done with all the planning that comes before your outline!

Check out your six-word memoir. Like it? Turn it around in your mind, hold it up to the light. Want to swap out some words? Go for it.

Now set it back down and look at your big personal change (also known as your character arc).

You're going to write your two-sentence elevator pitch, keeping your six-word memoir and your big personal change (your character arc) in mind. Refer to Nine of FDYM if you need examples. Yes, this is hard. But stand back and squint and see that you're doing something *really* exciting. You're writing the premise of the entire book, and then you'll write the book that will prove this premise true!

Write yours now, keeping in mind your six-word memoir and your character arc. Keep messing around with this. Shove the words to the right and then to the left. Make them dance on the page. Play. Explore. Brainstorm. Try to do this by yourself, if possible—know that this is *yours*. You don't have to tell a single person what you're planning to do.

Do this now, and don't spend more than fifteen minutes on it.

Ten

OUTLINE: THE MOST IMPORTANT PART OF YOUR PLAN

First, make a pot of tea. Or if you're more of a coffee person, brew up a carafe. Whatever shape your thinking cap is in, put it on your head.

It's go time.

You're going to outline your book now.

Ten chapters is a really great place to start, so we'll start there. You may end up with seven chapters when you're done, or you might have thirty-five. But ten is our jumping-off number.

Below, **next to the numbers,** write down some things that happened to you while moving from your early, unchanged self toward the self you want to show at the end of the book.

Don't write next to a) b) or c) yet!

Write down just the big events that mattered on *this particular* journey. Remember, you are not writing an autobiography!

Don't write down the big events of your whole life's journey! (Go back to Two of FDYM if you need a reminder of why it's so important that you *not* write an autobiography!)

Slap those events down in order, chronologically.

1. _____

    a. _____

    _____

    _____

    b. _____

    _____

    _____

    c. _____

    _____

    _____

2. _____

    a. _____

b.

c.

3.

    a.

    b.

c. _____

_____

_____

4. _____

a. _____

_____

_____

b. _____

_____

_____

c. _____

_____

_____

5. _____

   a. _____

      _____

      _____

   b. _____

      _____

      _____

   c. _____

      _____

      _____

6. _____

   a. _____

      _____

      _____

b. _____

_____

_____

c. _____

_____

_____

7. _____

    a. _____

_____

_____

    b. _____

_____

_____

    c. _____

8. _____

  a. _____

  b. _____

  c. _____

9. _____

  a. _____

b.

c.

10.

a.

b.

c. _____

Got your ten big events? (Or eight, or twelve? You're the boss!)

Next step: write down two or three smaller things that contributed to each big event that happened. See Ten of FDYM for examples. Remember, big events are *chapters,* and the significant moment events are *scenes.*

Go ahead and jot down those scenes now. It's totally okay if you have to leave some blanks, just like it's okay if you have more than three for each big event. You're playing right now.

Don't spend more than thirty minutes doing the first draft of this.

Let this exercise remind you that yes, you really *do* have a book in you.

You've got some scenes you think you could write. You might not have a full ten chapters with thirty scenes, but hey, if you've got even a few, that's a great starting point. And more will come to you as we go, I promise.

NOTE: we write these ideas down in chronological order, because it makes sense in our human brains. Often, we write the book in chrono-order, too. But *you don't have to.* If, when you get to the writing time, you want to jump around, you get to do that! And in revision, you might reorder the book completely! That's all good!

Onward!

Eleven

STORY STRUCTURE AND CHARACTER ARC

Let's rip apart that gorgeous outline you just made! Refer back to Eleven of FDYM if the idea of this freaks you out!

Stories require *structure.* It's literary gravity—your book has to have good structure in order to satisfy the reader.

The Four-Act Structure

INTRO	REACTION	ACTION	RESOLUTION
Intro Hero	Hero is a wanderer	Hero is a warrior	Hero wins
Intro hero, Setup and foreshadow stakes and quest	Hero reacts to the change resulting from first plot point	Hero is proactive as the antagonist ramps up	Hero steps up, steps in, confronts, resolves
Hook	First Plot Point aka Inciting Incident at 10–20%	Second Plot Point aka Context Shifting Midpoint at 50%	Third Plot Point aka Dark moment at 75–80%

4-Act Structure, adapted from Larry Brooks

Each of these boxes is *approximately* 25 percent of the length of the total book. Sometimes the first quarter and the last quarter are a little shorter than that, giving you more room in the second and third quarters.

The hero (that's you) has a different job in each box.

Sitting between the boxes are Big Things That Happen.

There. That's all it is. Four boxes: Introduction, Reaction, Action, Resolution.

So now your job is this: go through your outline with the four-act structure in mind. Don't forget: you must show your big personal change in your memoir.

Use these pages to brainstorm how you might *shape* this book of yours! I'm including three repeats, because as we write, we often change our minds about what the hook and those plot points might be. Feel free to play. To mess up! You probably won't figure this out in one sitting. Refer back to FDYM for lots more ideas.

Your Four-Act Structure

ACT 1: INTRODUCTION

ACT 2: REACTION

ACT 3: ACTION

ACT 4: RESOLUTION

ACT 1: INTRODUCTION

ACT 2: REACTION

ACT 3: ACTION

ACT 4: RESOLUTION

ACT 1: INTRODUCTION

ACT 2: REACTION

ACT 3: ACTION

ACT 4: RESOLUTION

Twelve

WRITING THE DAMN BOOK

IT IS TIME!

You're going to write this book scene by scene. It's that easy. Okay, and it's that hard, too—you already know that. But you're ready!

Each of the scenes in your book will fit into one of those four structural boxes we talked about.

But you might not actually know where those scenes fit yet. That's okay.

You do *not* have to write in chronological order, although many people, including myself, often do. Nope, you can write scenes from your outline in any order at all. Write what excites you! If you get bored writing a scene, STOP WRITING and write a different one! Follow your interest. If you can't wait to write that summer vacation morning memory, write it now. Move toward what you *want* to write.

Will this leave a mess behind you? Yes! And that means you're doing it right! Good job!

STARTING!

1. What's your word-count goal for this week? Just guesstimate this—it will change as you learn your best rhythms.

    _____

2. When and where will you write this week? Remember, people who make a plan of action including time and place are two to three times *more likely* to do the work!

    _____

    _____

    _____

    _____

3. How will you celebrate your first day of really writing?

    _____

    _____

    _____

    _____

4. How will you support yourself when you run headlong into the Gap, when your inner editor yells that you're not good enough to do this yet?

5. What will you tell yourself when the job seems too big for you to do?

6. Remind yourself: why does writing *this book* matter to you? This is your WHY, and knowing it is crucial to keep yourself going through the muddy middle.

Awesome work! Now you have a few tools to help you get your writing done! Bookmark these pages, or stick a Post-it on the most important ones. Come back here when you're feeling down, like you can't do it. You *can* do this. The doubt and difficulty are normal! These questions will help remind you of why you're taking this wild, wonderful adventure through your brain.

OPTIONAL QUESTIONS (but encouraged!)

1. It's amazing how we can quickly forget this decision of what to show in terms of character arc. You can't show how you became a brave mother, a selfless daughter, a powerful attorney, a compassionate philanthropist, *and* learned you were enough just as you are. That's too much! When you narrow down the focus of how you'll change in *this* memoir, you remind yourself that all the scenes you *could* write won't suit this book, even if they were amazing things that happened. (Save those for your next book!) You're only writing with *this focus*. So now, without flipping back to the previous pages, write again your character arc in this memoir. You're writing this book to show that you changed from *what* to *what*?

2. What's the ending?

It's probably the most recent thing to happen to you in your whole memoir. It will be easy to write. It's when you're finally standing in that true, changed self. Do you know it? When you have it, you'll have a pushpin on the map to show where you're heading. You'll spend the rest of your time in the book driving in the direction of this ending, and knowing your ending informs the rest of your writing.

So start now. Write a very, *very* rough skeletal draft of your ending right now. **It should be bad writing. Don't edit it.** Just write the last three or five paragraphs of your whole book. Where are you? What scene are you showing? What are you doing inside that scene? Is this where you handed your son the car keys, finally able to release control? Or when you chose your own fruit at the grocery store and felt a burst of joy radiate from under your skin?

GO!

How did that feel? Was it fun? Horrible? All experiences are welcome! Is the actual writing not that great? I hope so! I want you to feel the Gap and be okay with it. Your ending will change, I promise you. But that will be later, when you know and understand *this* book, after it teaches you what it wants to teach you.

I'm proud of you! Onward!

Thirteen

HOW TO GET OUT OF YOUR OWN WAY AND WRITE

1. Finding Time

Remember, in Fourteen of FDYM, I talked about how procrastination works, that you're handing a project off to someone your brain doesn't really accept as a real person. In my brain, and in yours, when we push something off to another day, we are expecting *someone we don't know* to pick up the slack later.

That's a really mean thing to do to yourself. So that stops now! Let's make some awesome, healthy plans!

1. When and where will you write?

You already made a plan for your first week—what about the next few weeks to a month? Writing time in our lives always changes, but I recommend you start with 30–45 minutes a day at first. Work your way up to a couple of hours of writing at a time if that's what you want, and remember, there's no hurry to get there! I still write most of my books in 45–60 minutes per day. That's all it takes!

Where will writing best fit into your life? Are you a morning, afternoon, or evening writer?

_____

_____

_____

_____

_____

_____

_____

2. What will you do if that chosen time doesn't work? (By *not working*, I mean you make a plan, and then you don't follow through. If you plan to write after work, and then you watch Netflix instead, then writing after work will

probably never work for you—where else can it fit in your life?)

_____

_____

_____

_____

_____

_____

3. Get out!

Where will you go? Can you get out of the house and write in a location you only use for writing? (Your car, the library, the local coffee house?) Or if you can't leave the house due to pandemic or kids or other extenuating circumstances, where in your house will you *only* write? Make it special, even if it's just the chair you never usually sit in at the dining table. Add a candle, or a nice place for your coffee to sit. Make it somewhere you don't pay the bills or answer email. Make it *your* writing place, the place where writing gets done. You can have multiple places! I love the library, and my couch—the end where I never sit to watch TV. It's my couch writing spot, and I've made it cozy with a "writing blanket" and a place for my mug.

Where is your place? Or places? How will you make them special, and just for writing?

4. Turn Off the Shiny

How will you mitigate distractions? Will you use something like Freedom.to to shut off the internet? Or disconnect your router while writing? Where will you store your phone so it's silent *and* out of your line of sight? (The University of Chicago did a study that proved our phones tax our cognition levels just by being in the same *room* with us, even if they're not visible.)

What's your plan?

5. What else will cue you that it's time to work? A playlist?
   A certain scent? A physical routine before you sit down? I
   like to stretch and do a couple of yoga moves that, because
   I always do them before I sit down to write, tell my body
   and brain that yes, it's time! What rituals can you put in
   place? List as many as you can think of!

6. Remember, if you say *I can't write fast because I have to make everything perfect before I move on,* that's fine ONLY if this method works for you AND you're completing books. In other words, if you're completing what you set out to complete, then yay! But if you want to write your memoir but are stymied because of the whole "perfection" thing, then you need to barrel through a really horrible first draft. Your method isn't working. Try a new one, friend. Try this one. So how will you keep reminding yourself that you're writing a crappy first draft?

SELF-CARE

Planning for Self-Care

I want you to plan for your self-care *before* you hit a rough patch. Refer to Fifteen of FDYM for my personal list of things I like to do for self-care, if you need a jumping off point.

What tools will you reach for when you need self-care while writing? List them here:

_____

_____

_____

_____

_____

Awesome job! Now you have *what* you'll do, but maybe even more importantly, how will you notice that you need a dollop of self-care? What will be your trigger to come back to this part of the book? Brainstorm here about what might send you to your self-care list (e.g., crying when writing, or avoiding the page even after you've promised yourself you'll write).

_____

_____

_____

_____

_____

_____

Who will you reach out to for help when you need it? Again, don't show them your work! But you'll need a kind ear or two on those hard days, people to whom you can say, "I'm writing about my history of abuse, and it's ripping me apart. Can we talk for thirty minutes? I just need a friend to listen." Who can you trust with this task of listening?

_____

_____

_____

_____

_____

NOTE: if you don't have anyone to put on that list, that's okay. That's really normal! But you're going to *need* to put someone on it if your book has trauma or shame in it. And every good memoir will usually have at least one moment of real, deep pain. Remember, no one wants to read the "I'm So Awesome" memoir.

So, if no one in your life is safe enough to share this with, it's time to hire someone to be put on this list. Google for therapists in your area, and check their reviews and ratings. If you're broke, visit a site like Open Path Psychotherapy Collective, which offers affordable in-office and online psychotherapy sessions. Set this workbook down, and get thee to Google, right now! YOU DESERVE SUPPORT, and by writing your memoir, you're going to trigger some old stuff. Put on your life preserver (and that's what it is, truly) *before* wading into the deep water.

What else should you do to take care of yourself while writing this book?

Fifteen

WRITING MEDITATION

Don't skip this step! The results may (and probably will) surprise you!

The first thing you're going to do is make a commitment to simply trying this weird brain exercise. Remember, when you meditate, you are *literally* doing push-ups for your brain. Doing a bit of meditation every day will make you a better and more resilient writer, and that's an amazing outcome from just sitting around!

So grab your pen, and let's get started. I'll have some questions for you to think about after your session.

Here's a reminder of the three simple steps to secular meditation (see FDYM Sixteen for more detail):

1. **Sit or lie down.**
2. **Think about your breath.**
3. **Get distracted.**

Then just repeat steps three and four, toggling between focusing on your breath and getting distracted.

Okay! Are you comfy? You don't have to sit on a meditation cushion—your couch or desk chair or the floor of the living room will work just fine. It's okay if animals bounce on and off your lap.

Set the timer on your phone for five minutes. And. . . GO!

5 MIN

Welcome back!

Remember that meditation is *not* about clearing the mind and getting calm! The magic of meditation is the Getting-Distracted part. It's okay if you feel you got nothing out of that exercise. Because, honestly, you did. Even if you felt like it was just five minutes of making shopping lists, it was actually more than that. Your brain just got a teensy bit stronger.

1. What did that experience feel like? Describe what happened inside your body and inside your brain.

2. Are you happy or frustrated with this exercise? (There are no wrong answers.) What does *that* feel like?

3. Did you get good and distracted? If so, congratulate yourself here!

4. Make a plan with a time and place for trying
   again tomorrow.

Give meditation fourteen days, at least, before you decide
whether you'll continue with it. You're getting a stronger mind!
You may only be able to do a couple of push-ups at first, but
if you meditate a tiny bit again tomorrow, your brain will be
getting stronger and happier (literally).

Meditation makes you a stronger, better writer, one who
has an easier time both getting to the page and staying there for
longer periods!

Advanced (Optional) Tactic

Don't forget, you can use meditation to pull out memories!
Want to try it?

Meditate for a while, as described above, for maybe three
to ten minutes.

Then, when you're ready, imagine a room in your past you'd
like to revisit to look for memories. Spend a few minutes just
wandering around it, touching things in your mind, pulling
open doors or drawers. Keep moving around the room. Once
you stub your toe on a memory, play with it in your mind. At
this point, let your brain get distracted. It's okay to follow your
thoughts around. You might fly off to the underground Paris

nightclub where you met the man who would become your husband. Walk around that room now. What was on the walls? Be okay with not being able to remember, but be open to being surprised by how much you can recall in this meditative state.

What did you see? What did you remember that you'd totally forgotten?

Sixteen

PRESERVE MEMORY MOVING FORWARD

Now, my friend, as you begin this work, you are a memoirist! You really are one, no matter whether your book is done or published yet.

YOU ARE A WRITER! You are a memoirist!

And even though you might not believe it right now, writing memoir is more addictive than it says on the package. What if you get hooked? What if, someday, you want to write about your life right now?

What crumbs of memory are you losing by not catching them?

So grab your favorite pen and answer these questions:

1. Have you journaled in the past? If so, what did you gain from it, and why did you stop? If you're still a journaler, what do you get from it?

2. What keeps you from journaling?

3. Take a few minutes and think about yesterday. Walk yourself through the day, from the moment you awoke until you went to bed. Use your calendar if you need to refresh your memory. Try to find one single moment in it that might make a good little story. It can be the smile the cashier gave you (but she still looked sad) or the way your kid screamed bloody murder when he caught his brother with an extra cookie. Write about that moment right here. (Remember—it's a first draft, so it's supposed to be bad, and it's technically a *journal* entry, so it can be extra terrible! Just get it out.) Try to fill all three pages here.

_____

_____

_____

_____

_____

4. Think again about the Annie Dillard quote, "How we
    spend our days is, of course, how we spend our lives."
    What's the best way for you to catch how you're spending
    your days? Is it journaling? Is it keeping a Google Doc
    with one sentence a day about what happened? Brainstorm
    some ideas that might work for you to honor your new
    memoirist persona!

_____

_____

_____

_____

_____

Seventeen

PRACTICING THE PRO TIPS!

Let's practice some of those big writing hacks I shared with you in Eighteen of FDYM. Don't worry—you can't get this wrong. Shake out your shoulders and wrists, and let your jaw relax a little. Now, let's play!

Visceral Emotions

Rewrite and expand the following sentence it in your own words. Look back into your life, find a time you felt this way, and restate it, using *physical details about your body* in order to bring the reader right into the way you felt. Try not to say the word "ashamed." Show it in your body, instead. Revisit Eighteen in FDYM if you need to for some tips on how and why this is important!

I felt ashamed.

Specific Senses

Practice using specific senses here (refer to FDYM for examples). Lean into sights, smells, sounds, touch, and even taste, if you can wedge it in there! If you can't think of a time in your life when you were amazed that a room was transformed, write this as fiction—this is just practice, after all. If you *can* think of a time, write about that, and use the 80% rule to put down specifics that you're pretty sure of. Maybe you can't *quite* remember the scent of chai hanging in the air, but because your auntie was there, you're pretty darn sure that she'd made some. Write it down! BE SPECIFIC! Try not to use the word "amazed."

I was amazed at how the room had transformed.

_____

_____

_____

_____

_____

_____

Extra credit: now write a line or two about how it felt, viscerally, to be inside your body when you viewed the room's transformation.

_____

_____

_____

_____

_____

Dialogue

Let's practice writing dialogue! Use this space to expand a memory of when someone once told you to leave. Maybe grab a line or two someone said just before you were told to get out, and then add what you said in response. It's okay that you can't remember the exact words anyone said. What's important is getting the dialogue on the page. Dialogue makes the scene come alive! Try not to use the words "couldn't believe" (can you show that in your body in a visceral way?) or the words "told me."

I couldn't believe it when (s)he told me to leave.

_____

_____

_____

_____

_____

_____

_____

Take a moment and reread what you wrote. Amazing, right? Compare it to the simple and *boring*, "I couldn't believe it when (s)he told me to leave." How much more exciting is yours than the original? Great job!

Extra credit: call a relative. Have a chat. Do not record it, and don't try too hard to memorize what's discussed. As soon as you hang up, write a few notes to yourself about what was said, and more importantly, what was implied without words. Expand this into a scene. You don't have to use this in your memoir (in fact, you probably won't), but while you write the scene, pretend you will. Include only the info that gets your meaning across.

Point of View

Put simply, you've got to stay in your own lane. As a memoirist, you can only describe what *you* know. If you say, "I was scared," we can believe you. (But show us viscerally, huh?) If you say, "Mom was scared," then you *must* show us why you believe that. Either she can tell you that in dialogue, or you can extrapolate it from physical clues, but you can't head-hop into her point of view (POV). If you enter Mom's POV, you're making something up out of whole cloth, and even if you're right about how she feels, it's technically a lie. Don't lie to your reader. They'll know and close the book forever.

Here's an example for you to clean up. Obviously, it's not from *your* memoir, but the practice of doing it will help you sort out how to do this in your own work.

I couldn't believe my sister hadn't told me she was going out for the evening. I shouted, "What do you mean, you're leaving?"

My sister believed I was overreacting. She thought about how I always got offended when things weren't run past me. "I'll be back in a few hours—stop overreacting!"

My brother felt a chill go through him. That was when he knew she wasn't ever going to come home again.

All I could do was throw a dishtowel at her retreating back as I shouted, "Just go, then!"

Wrestle this out for a fix. I know it can be hard. Think of the ways you can make this *only* from the "I" character's point of view. Think about words like, "apparently" or "I imagined that," etc. Bring it all back to that main character, the only point of view we get in a memoir.

_____

_____

_____

_____

_____

_____

Tense

Whew, an easy one! What do you feel more drawn to? Present or past tense?

_____

If you're having a hard time deciding what you like best, I find the most useful thing is to go to your bookshelf or Kindle and pull up your most recent favorite memoirs. Dive into random spots and figure out what they're doing. Why do you like it?

OR: just write. The tense will work itself out as you go, and you'll decide what you like best. It's okay to slip around for a while, moving in and out of past and present tense. First drafts are messy! And you're doing great!

Eighteen

WORRY BUSTING

Here's where you get to do a little more worry-busting on your own. I want you to respond to yourself here. You can always refer back to this in FDYM if you want to see how I responded to these worries, but try not to, until you have some crappy first-draft answers right here. Ask your brilliant, inspired self—that deep, gut-level version of the best you—to talk to your worried self.

Of course, if the statement doesn't apply to you, skip it! There's a spot at the end to write down your biggest worry if I haven't hit it here.

I'm not a good enough writer to do this. I'm a fraud.

_____

_____

_____

_____

_____

_____

_____

I don't have enough story. Everyone else was lost on a mountain/hideously abused/a war hero, but all I have is a story about _____. No drama. It's going to be so boring!

_____

_____

_____

_____

_____

_____

_____

_____

_____

I'm worried I won't follow through and finish.

_____

_____

_____

_____

_____

_____

_____

_____

I'm scared of failing.

People will hate me if I write this stuff.

_____

_____

_____

_____

_____

_____

I'm supposed to write a crappy first draft and revise it later, but I don't know how to revise.

_____

_____

_____

_____

_____

_____

_____

I've started, but I've lost my mojo. I don't think I'll get it back.

Over to you! Write your worry (or worries) that I didn't hit here and then have your gorgeous gut instinct answer them reassuringly.

_____

_____

_____

_____

_____

_____

_____

_____

_____

_____

Maybe stick a little Post-it bookmark in this chapter, too. You'll want to come back here!

∽∽∽∽

REVISION

Hello! Are you still writing your first draft? Then there's nothing for you to do in this chapter! Just skip it and come back when your first draft is a glorious, sloppy, impossible-to-understand, and completed mess!

Oh!

Hello! You're back! With your completed manuscript in hand? Good for you! Sit right down and grab your pen.

Don't worry—this is going to be *way* more fun than you can even imagine! Revision is when the *really* big ideas show up. Then you move parts around—like those flat puzzle toys where you slide pieces around to make a picture—to make the new ideas fit. You might have to pry out some pieces and manufacture new ones. But then you click one piece left and another one right, and suddenly, you're looking at it. You see the whole picture. Your book.

Okay, revision is really hard, too. (I actually teach a 90-day course in revision—you can always go to rachaelherron.com/revision to see if I have a section of it coming up anytime soon. Revision is a great thing to do with a hand to hold.)

Macro Revision

Find Your Theme

We talked a lot about writing either a time-based or a theme-based memoir. This is *not* the same kind of theme (ah, those tricky writing words that serve multiple purposes). When I say "theme" here, I mean the overall message of your book. Now that your first draft is done, I want you to find a simple theme that defines what you're trying to pull off with this memoir. I want you to be able to encapsulate your entire book in just a few words.

Examples

Love heals all wounds.
Love heals no wounds.
Family is strongest when chosen.
Pain leads to growth.

What's your theme for this memoir? Write it down now. If you'd like your reader to take away one universal statement about the way you look at the world, what would that be?

_____

_____

_____

_____

_____

_____

Got it? (It can change later if it needs to!) Now write it on a small Post-it and smack it onto the top of your computer!

Now go back to FDYM to follow the next instructions about how to print out the book and how to read it. After you've done that, it's time for…

The Sentence Outline

Jot down a phrase for each scene that will remind you of what happened in it. See FDYM for examples. No one has to understand this code but you!

You might want to do this in Scrivener or a Google doc, or by hand in your journal (that's what I always do), but in case you want to do it in this workbook, please use the following pages! I'm giving you 100 lines for 100 scenes—if your book has more than that, you'll have to do this assignment elsewhere. I usually have about 50 scenes for a 90,000-word book, but that's just my mileage, yours will vary. And yes, I'm only giving you one line per scene! Your phrase should be short enough to fit on one line!

SENTENCE OUTLINE:

1. _____

2. _____

3. _____

4. _____

5. _____

6. _____

7. _____

8. _____

9. _____

10. _____

11. _____

12. _____

13. _____

14. _____

15. _____

16. _____

17. _____

18. _____

19. _____

20. _____

21. _____

22. _____

23. _____

24. _____

25. _____

26. _____

27. _____

28. _____

29. _____

30. _____

31. _____

32. _____

33. _____

34. _____

35. _____

36. _____

37. _____

38. _____

39. _____

40. _____

41. _____

42. _____

43. _____

44. _____

45. _____

46. _____

47. _____

48. _____

49. _____

50. _____

51. _____

52. _____

53. _____

54. _____

55. _____

56. _____

57. _____

58. _____

59. _____

60. _____

61. _____

62. _____

63. _____

64. _____

65. _____

66. _____

67. _____

68. _____

69. _____

70. _____

71. _____

72. _____

73. _____

74. _____

75. _____

76. _____

77. _____

78. _____

79. _____

80. _____

81. _____

82. _____

83. _____

84. _____

85. _____

86. _____

87. _____

88. _____

89. _____

90. _____

91. _____

92. _____

93. _____

94. _____

95. _____

96. _____

97. _____

98. _____

99. _____

100. _____

Post-its!

See FDYM for instructions – if you're using this book for your sentence outline, then keep your Post-its right here for now! I recommend the 1.5 × 2-inch kind, and you can stack quite a few on these next six pages. Use this as your starting Post-it lily pad!

POST-ITS

POST-ITS

POST-ITS

POST-ITS

POST-ITS

POST-ITS

You're Ready to Start!

You're now 99 percent more equipped than most writers are when they stare into the open maw of revision. Take a moment to feel proud of that fact. Feel your chest swell.

Now the real fun begins.

Print out that list of scenes, your sentence outline. (If you've been writing this by hand, that's fine, but quick-like-a-bunny type it up now, double-spaced.)

Read it.

There.

You just took about two minutes to read your entire book.

And I bet you're feeling some things. You realize that the back end of the book is too heavy with stories about your husband, whereas you want this to be more about you and your mom. Or you see that you need more about basic training and Iraq and less about Afghanistan.

Even better, while reading, you make an association you've never seen before. Oh, shit, the problem you had at that job was directly related to the problem you had as an eight-year-old on the playground! How could you not have seen that before now?

Draw all over it. Mark it up. Draw arrows. Write bubbles of dialogue you hear in your head. Make connections.

Look at the story structure again and think about those four boxes. See if you can slide scenes around to help you create a stronger story arc. Keep in mind those turning points—see if you can find them in your outline.

- Can you find the 20–25 percent mark, when something took you out of your normal routine, pushing you into Reaction?
- Can you find the 50 percent context-shifting midpoint when you moved into Action?
- Can you find the 75–80 percent Dark Moment when all was lost?

Mark these on your sentence outline. Remember, it's totally okay to retype this sentence outline and move things around if you want to!

Are multiple timelines confusing you? See FDYM for more help.

When you're done with your new outline, you have a map for your revisions.

You're ready to start revising!

And yes, it's normal to be REALLY confused at this point. That's okay. We do the work anyway, and things *will* get clearer as you go. Reread this section in FDYM and GO! You can do it!

The Draft Passes

After you've done one big revision (the biggest, hardest one!), and *after* you feel like your book's scenes make sense where they are, only then is it time to come back to the draft passes.

If you're at that point, first, YAY YOU and second, grab a cup of coffee and ask yourself these questions to find out where your weaknesses are.

YES NO

❏ ❏ **Dialogue:** Is it strong? Does it occur often enough? Do the different characters' voices sound clear enough?

❏ ❏ **Characters:** Is your change as a character clear enough?

❏ ❏ **Visceral details:** Can the reader feel the main character's emotions simply through bodily, visceral details?

❏ ❏ **Point of view:** Do you always stay in the "I" character's point of view?

❏ ❏ **Tense:** Is the tense consistent?

❏ ❏ **Transitions:** Is there a smooth connection between each scene?

❏ ❏ **Passive voice:** Is your manuscript mostly clear of the passive voice?

❏ ❏ **Setting:** As mentioned, are we solidly in the world? Can we see, hear, taste, smell, touch the environment?

❏ ❏ **Truthfulness:** Is this as true as you can make it, using the 80% Rule?

❏ ❏ **Humor:** If your book needs it, is there enough humor?

❏ ❏ **Seriousness:** If your book needs it, is there enough seriousness?

If you checked NO to any of these, then that's a pass you'll be doing! I often check all of them, myself. Some passes are quick—I can fix transitions between scenes in a few hours. Others, like character arc, might take days of work. But each time you go back into the work, you're *just* looking for that one bugaboo at a time. It makes it so much easier to knit the whole together.

NOTE: this is not a comprehensive list! If you have a personal weakness that's not on this list, add it as a draft pass.

Micro Revision

See FDYM for more—this is when you finally get to make every sentence sing! Each scene has now earned its place in the book, so now you get to make each sentence earn its keep, too! I love this part most of all, and I bet you will, too.

Finally, Your Book is Done!

How will you celebrate?

_____

_____

_____

_____

_____

Twenty

HOW TO PUBLISH

This is a quick section, since this book isn't about the publishing industry. See 21 of FDYM for all my recommendations.

But do take a moment to think about what you *want*. Do you want to be traditionally published? Does the idea of self-publishing excite you? What are you more drawn to, right now?

_____

_____

_____

_____

_____

Given what you're thinking about, what's your next step? Will you hire a developmental editor so that you can self-publish? Or will you search for an agent? Or will you hire a developmental editor *before* you search for an agent? (I recommend Reedsy for hiring editors who are independent contractors and fully vetted. I believe in Reedsy so much I actually asked them for an affiliate link: Rachaelherron.com/reedsy.) What are the pros and cons of each of these? This is a YOU decision. How do you feel?

_____

_____

_____

_____

_____

Most importantly, how do you feel now that you've finished a book and you're ready to send it into the world to stand on its own two feet? It's okay if you feel weird about it, or half-happy, half-sad. All feelings are welcome. What's going on in your head now?

_____

_____

_____

_____

_____

OH MY GOSH, YOU DID IT! I'm SO proud of you!

❧❧❧

Twenty-One

THE LAST WORD

There's nothing for you to write here. I'm just going to reprint the last from FDYM in its entirety, so you can remember what you did and who you are.

Dearest memoirist (because you get to call yourself that, you know),

Your story matters.

The world needs it.

There is no one but *you* who can write your story. There are people desperate to know that they can make it through what they're going through, the thing you conquered. Your book could save their lives.

Or perhaps your book is a little quieter—maybe it will make someone forget that they're in a hospital bed. Maybe they'll laugh while reading what *you* wrote. What greater honor is there than that—to distract a worried and heavy mind? How worthy and how magnificent a gift is that to give someone?

And the one thing I know for sure is this: I can't put together sentences like you can. No one in the whole world can—not one person who's ever lived on this planet has *your* unique sensibilities and your ability to craft words into phrases, sentences, paragraphs, pages, and finally, into BOOKS.

I want you to do this.

I don't want you to read this book and become inspired and then fail to launch.

I want you to do the work.

> Louis L'Amour said, "Start writing, no matter what. The water doesn't flow until you turn on the faucet."

It's hard work! I've made that damn clear, haven't I? Sorry about that. But you've learned I value truth, and you would think less of me if I lied to you about this.

But writing is the *best* work that exists. I think firefighting and midwifery are incredible jobs, but even an astronaut's job doesn't hold a single itty-bitty candle to the job we get to do when we sit at the page and tell our stories.

The ability and the desire to write came to you for a reason. **You're burdened with this desire because you have a story to tell.**

So go write it. Then share it.
We want to read it.
And when you do publish it? Let me know, would you?
I can't wait to see what you do.
With all my heart, I say,
Onward!

ABOUT RACHAEL

Official Biography

Rachael Herron is the internationally bestselling author of more than two dozen books, including memoir, thriller (under R.H. Herron), mainstream fiction, feminist romance, and nonfiction about writing. She received her MFA in writing from Mills College, Oakland, and she teaches writing extension workshops at both UC Berkeley and Stanford. She is a proud member of the NaNoWriMo Writer's Board. She's a New Zealand citizen as well as an American.

Writing Group

Do join my writing email list! Every week, I send out an encouraging email, totally free, nudging you to *do the work* that matters most to you. It's a free, very friendly ass-kicking. Go to rachaelherron.com/write to sign up.

Coaching

I offer 30-minute publishing consultations over Zoom. (This is the perfect time to run your outline by someone or to ask any questions that remain about memoir or any other part of the writing craft.) You also get the mp3 of our talk, so you don't have to scribble notes till your hand cramps. See more at rachaelherron.com/coach.

Teaching

> **"Rachael is one of the few speakers we've ever had at our conferences who has received a perfect score in one of our post-event surveys for her session.** In short, she resonates with our audience. And not just because she knows her stuff—she does—or because she's hilarious—she is—but because her honesty and earnestness come through in all her messaging."
>
> —Samantha Sanders, Writer's Digest

Bring me to your writing group, your retreat, your Rotary club, whatever you'd like. I can teach this book in as little as two hours and up to a full-day (or two) course.

Email me for details. Rachael@rachaelherron.com.

Made in the USA
Monee, IL
09 March 2022

92586377R00108